CORVETTE

YESTERDAY & TODAY ™

THE AUTO EDITORS OF CONSUMER GUIDE®

Publications International, Ltd.

Credits

Photography:

The editors would like to thank the following people and organizations for supplying the photography that made this book possible. They are listed below, along with the page number(s) of their photos.

Dave Arnold: 114, 115; **Mark Elias:** 24, 29, 66, 96, 97, 126; **Mitch Frumkin:** 98, 128; **Thomas Glatch:** 31, 35, 64, 79, 126, 156; **Sam Griffith:** 8, 44, 67, 68, 96, 125, 135, 138, 158; **Brandon Hemphill:** 27, 32, 36, 66, 96, 97; **Bud Juneau:** 18, 40, 98, 112; **Harry Kapsalis:** 69; **Milton Kieft:** 65, 95, 125, 155; **Bill Kilborn:** 94; **Erik Lesser/GM Media:** 56; **Dan Lyons:** Front cover, 23, 65, 66, 67, 96, 97, 113; **Vince Manocchi:** 10, 12, 15, 16, 30, 32, 33, 37, 64, 65, 66, 67, 94, 95, 96, 97, 104, 124, 125, 126, 127, 132, 133, 155, 156; **Ron McQueeney:** 107; **Doug Mitchel:** 17, 18, 23, 25, 26, 28, 51, 95, 96, 98, 128, 135, 141, 155, 156, 158; **Mike Mueller:** 13, 65, 67, 97, 125; **Neil Nissing:** 49, 65, 128; **Nina Padgett:** 31; **Dorsey Patrick/GM Racing:** 146; **Richard Prince/GM Racing:** 101, 119, 120, 121, 122, 123; **Nina Russin:** 137; **Tom Storm:** 12; **David Temple:** 19, 22; **Phil Toy:** 74; **W. C. Waymack:** 16, 19, 32, 95, 97, 155; **F. Pierce Williams/GM Media:** 143

Owners:

Special thanks to the owners of the cars featured in this book for their cooperation.

Robert and Diane Adams: 16; **Mark Alter:** 32, 65, 126; **John Baritel:** 125; **Ralph and Carol Barton:** 97; **Biff Behr and Lynne Richman:** 18, 95, 155; **Benchmark Classics:** 35; **Lon and Barbara Berger:** 12, 95; **Les Bieri and John Angwert:** 64; **Jim Blanchard:** 16, 65; **Pete Bogard:** 15; **Dorothy Clemmer:** 64, 67, 94, 124, 132; **Larry Coleman:** 19; **Patrick and Kay Collins:** 30, 126; **Corvette Mike:** 37, 97; **Thomas and Mae Crockatt:** 96; **Allen Cummins:** 96; **Jeff Dranson:** 13; **John M. Endres:** 40, 98; **Ray Fecteau:** 23; **David L. Ferguson:** 10, 95, 125; **Marvin Friedman:** 156; **Shawn Friedman:** 25; **Gateway Classic Cars:** 32; **Jack Gersh:** 156; **Gary A. Girt:** 65, 95, 125, 155; **Dave and Mary Glass:** 135; **Eric P. Goodman:** 17, 95; **Fred Grasseschi:** Front cover; **Dr. Ernie Hendry:** 94; **J. Bruce Jacobs:** 96; **Joe D. James:** 19; **John E. and Barbara E. James:** 31; **Roger Judski:** 24, 29, 66, 96, 97, 126; **Robert Kleckauskas:** 96, 125; **Barry L. Klinkel:** 126; **Tom Korbas:** 25; **Edward S. Kuziel:** 125; **Donald Maich:** 18; **Rich Mason:** 104; **Dr. Milt McMillen:** 156; **Werner Meier:** 79; **Ed Milas:** 31, 126; **Edward L. Mueller:** 113; **Northwest Auto Sales:** 27, 36, 66, 96, 97; **Edward E. Ortiz:** 67, 127, 133; **Dr. Dennis Pagliano:** 15, 65, 95, 125; **Robert Paterson:** 112; **Jim Patterson:** 26; **Nelson Roach:** 22; **Roanoke Motor Co. Inc./William Clark:** 135; **Rick Robinson:** 32; **Tom Schay:** 8, 65, 96, 125, 155; **Alfred W. Schwacke:** 12; **Kamal Sharma:** 74; **Chuck Swafford:** 19; **Phil Trifaro:** 23, 66; **Carlos and Sherry Vivas:** 96; **Rosalie and Jim Wente:** 16, 95, 155; **Chip Werstein:** 65; **Rosanne Winney:** 33, 127; **Mike and Laurie Yager:** 28, 66, 96

Our appreciation to the historical archives and media services groups at General Motors Company.

About The Auto Editors of Consumer Guide®:

For more than 40 years, Consumer Guide® has been a trusted provider of new-car buying information.

The Consumer Guide® staff drives and evaluates more than 200 vehicles annually.

Consumerguide.com is one of the Web's most popular automotive resources, visited by roughly three million shoppers monthly.

The Auto Editors of Consumer Guide® also publish the award-winning bimonthly *Collectible Automobile®* magazine.

Contents

Welcome to *Corvette: Yesterday and Today*™, a complete, concise look at Chevrolet's superstar sports car. Since you're perusing this book, it's likely you're a Corvette fan and already know something about the cars. Perhaps you even own one. If so, you're in good company. The Corvette has been with us nearly 60 years now, and more than a million and a half have been sold. Such long-lived popularity is rare in the auto business, and it's why the 'Vette remains a hot topic for magazine articles and all kinds of books, including several from the editors of this volume. It's also the passion of at least five major clubs in the U.S. and millions of other devotees around the globe.

But if the Corvette scarcely needs introduction, there are a few things we'd like to point out by way of introduction to the colorful, multifaceted story that unfolds in these pages.

To begin with, the Corvette is not America's only bona fide sports car, nor even the first, but it is the most successful. It's certainly survived the longest, outlasting two-seaters with far less charisma from other automakers and even parent General Motors. Some see the Dodge Viper as a close rival, but it didn't come along until 1992, and the current model is slated to go out of production after 2010.

That leads to a second point. Although the Corvette has changed enormously through its six design generations to date, it's stayed remarkably consistent in several ways. It's always had a front-mounted engine, rear-wheel drive, and a lightweight "plastic" body—fiberglass into the late 1990s, high-tech composites since then. And except for the first two model years, 1953-54, Corvettes have been motivated by lusty V-8 engines, mostly the landmark "small-block" design that has also powered countless Chevrolet passenger cars and whose basic engineering principles live on in today's potent, efficient Corvette powerplants.

Which segues neatly to point three. As a specialty item selling in relatively modest numbers, the Corvette has always been a more cost-effective testbed for new GM technology, features, and production processes than a mass-market model would be, making innovation another longtime 'Vette hallmark. To name just a few examples: fuel injection (1957); independent rear suspension (1963); T-bar roof (1968); "virtual" instrumentation (1984); multivalve cylinder heads and tire-pressure monitor (1989); a rear-mounted transmission and a host of first-time materials applications such as a hydroformed-steel frame (1997); and the use of carbon fiber for certain body panels (2009).

Besides steadily advancing the state of technical arts, the Corvette has also embodied GM's most daring design ideas. Though the car's styling has changed dramatically over the decades, every Corvette was considered a knockout in its day and catches the eye even now. This, too, reflects a remarkable consistency. The look is always low and wide, with a long hood, bobbed tail, artfully shaped curves and creases, and interesting details galore. And though Corvette remains a fairly large sports car by world standards, its size reflects the bold, all-American persona that's another part of the car's appeal.

It's striking how a car with so much heart and soul could emerge from a big, profit-driven corporation like General Motors. But then, Corvettes have never been birthed like other GM cars. Each new generation has mainly been the work of relatively small groups of talented, enthusiastic designers, engineers, and managers who regard the Corvette as a plum assignment, a highlight of their careers. You'll see them mentioned throughout this book, as they deserve to be.

Racing looms large in the lore of many great sports cars. Corvette is no exception, so this book includes a chapter on that aspect of the story. Another section covers sought-after "special edition" models and pace cars. Here, too, is a look at the show cars, concepts, and fascinating one-of-a-kind customs that fueled enthusiast dreams by exploring new ideas for Corvette's future. You'll also find facts and photos on plans for production models that would never be.

All this and more awaits you in the pages that follow. We hope you enjoy this telling of an automotive success story that not only remains endlessly fascinating but seems destined to continue for many years to come, a happy prospect indeed.

C1
1953-1962

The Chevrolet Corvette got off to a whirlwind first year in 1953, having gone from GM Motorama show car to production status in just months. However, those early 'Vettes were more show than go, and the pricey roadster floundered in the marketplace. The car came close to being canceled before finding its stride in 1956 as a true sporting machine, and sales kept climbing through the end of its first generation.

All first-year Corvettes came painted Polo White with a Sportsman Red interior. Long, thin bumper blades aligned with the bodyside chrome spears to give the impression of a single band of chrome around the car broken only by the wheel openings, grille, and twin exhaust outlets. The short exhaust tips tended to discolor the paint. Corvette's fiberglass body comprised 46 separate pieces glued together to form nine major subassemblies—large jigs were used to position the individual pieces to assure proper fit. Fiberglass made for a much lighter car than traditional steel construction and could be more easily molded into complex shapes, like the floorpan shown at left. The lone powerplant was a 235.5-cid "Blue Flame" six that produced 150 hp. Because the engine was deemed too strong for Chevy's manual gearbox, a two-speed Powerglide automatic was the only transmission available.

1954

Corvette was little changed for 1954, but the body color palette expanded to include Pennant Blue, Sportsman Red, and black. Chevrolet dropped the advertised base price to $2774, though that was a bit misleading because previously standard items were now optional. A fully optioned 1954 'Vette left the actual price basically unchanged: $3254.10. Production was moved to a plant in St. Louis (right) that was capable of much higher volume than the temporary line in Flint—up to 10,000 units a year versus only 600. However, the extra capacity didn't matter—Chevrolet ended up building just 3640, many of which were unsold at year's end.

1955

Only 700 Corvettes were built for 1955, but nearly all of them packed Chevy's brilliant new small-block V-8, which was signaled by an exaggerated "V" in the bodyside Chevrolet script. A three-speed manual transmission was added late in the model year. For '56, Corvettes got revamped bodywork that included new headlights, twin hood bulges, fender-top scoops, inset taillights, and handsome bodyside coves. Contrasting paint in those coves was a $19.40 option. A lift-off hardtop was a new option, and roll-up windows were now included (previous 'Vettes made do with snap-in side curtains). And for the little tykes, a mini-Corvette pedal car was available. The 1956 models marked a key transformation in the Corvette's character and focus, as Chevrolet corrected the car's mechanical shortcomings and made it into a true sports car.

1956

CHEVROLET UNLEASHES THE NEW CORVETTE

Get set for the new Corvette. Get set for a new sight in sports car style and silhouette. Get set for a new sound, a new sensation, a new spirit-lifting surge of the Corvette's dynamic new 225-hp V8 engine. Get set, too, for new Corvette convenience—with new roll-up windows, a custom choice of standard power-operated fabric top or optional convertible hard-top, Powerglide or Synchro-Mesh transmission, and beautiful new colors and interiors. There's more—a new competition racing steering wheel, side-by-side bucket seats, and instrumentation as complete as a light plane's. But excitement is as excitement does. And you'll never know that till you drive it! . . . Chevrolet Division of General Motors, Detroit 2, Mich.

by Chevrolet

1957

Corvettes saw no visual changes for 1957, but plenty of mechanical improvements. The V-8 grew to 283 cubes, and a four-speed manual transmission became available late in the model year. Carbureted 'Vettes ranged in horsepower from 220 to 270, but the big news was the new Ramjet fuel injection. The topline solid-lifter "fuelie" V-8 produced 283 hp, achieving the benchmark of one horsepower per cubic inch. 'Vettes equipped with fuel injection wore scripts on their side coves and decklid, as well as bodyside crossed-flag emblems. 'Vette advertising developed a pronounced swagger this year, gleefully poking fun at European sports-car "purists." Like it or not, an American machine had officially arrived on the scene.

"FANTASTICO! EVEN IN TURIN NO ONE HAS FUEL INJECTION!"

Si, è vero. But the really fantastic item about the new Corvette is not the fuel injection engine, the new *four-speed gearbox,** the slingshot acceleration or the pasted-to-the-road stability. It is the fact that the Corvette, *above all other high-performance sports cars in the world,* is a true dual-natured vehicle. It is a genuine luxury car and a genuine sports car, both wrapped in one sleek skin.

This is something like a panther with a St. Bernard's disposition. Quite a trick, but *what a pet!* But, in case you may have polite doubts about the Corvette's uniqueness, we have an easy rebuttal: Drive one!

In point of fact, we have no further enticement. If you can spend half an hour in the deep-cushioned comfort of a Corvette's cockpit, if you can sample the crispness of its controls, the veracity of its 16 to 1 steering, the incredible crescendo of its performance—and remain unshaken—you are mighty close to being unique. Frankly, very few drivers escape the feeling that this is one of the authentic great moments of motoring—and those few are not warm to the touch! ... *Chevrolet Division of General Motors, Detroit 2, Michigan.*

CORVETTE
by Chevrolet

SPECIFICATIONS: 283-cubic-inch V8 engine with single four-barrel carburetor, 220 h.p. (four other engines* range to 283 h.p. with fuel injection). Close-ratio three-speed manual transmission standard, with special Powerglide automatic drive* available on all but maximum-performance engines. Choice of removable hard top or power-operated fabric top.* Power-Lift windows.* Instruments include 6000 r.p.m. tachometer, oil pressure gauge and ammeter. *Optional at extra cost.*

1958-1959

WHAT MAKES YOU THINK IT BURNS CHAMPAGNE?

It doesn't, of course. But the first time you buckle yourself behind the spring-steel wheel of a Corvette you're going to swear that something more exotic than mere gasoline is fueling that V8.

There's such a tremendous *elation* in the way a Corvette strides down the road, such a bubbly, tingling, let's-do-something aliveness about the way it responds. If it were nothing but a "straight-line" car, the full-throated sound and surge of that free-breathing V8 alone would be worth the price of admission. But when you wed that cyclone-breeder to a pure sports car chassis, to the sticks-like-glue stability of real sports car suspension, you've got a road machine that will spoil you for anything else, ever!

Have you driven a Corvette? Have you ever flicked that *all-synchro* four-speed gearbox down into Low for engine braking just before a hairpin corner? Have you ever gripped a wheel that translates the exact "feel" of the road to your fingers? If the answers are "no," we sincerely envy you. Check your Chevrolet dealer. He's got an Experience waiting for you—and that's a capital E!

CORVETTE by Chevrolet
. . . Chevrolet Division of General Motors, Detroit 2, Michigan

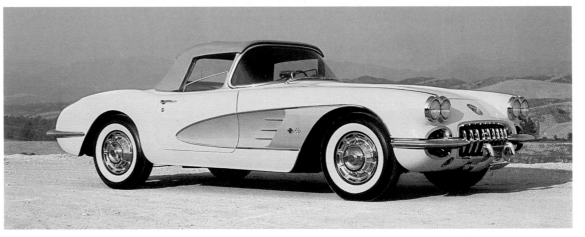

1960

for ten seconds try to imagine what owning a Corvette would be like . . .

you're close, but it's __better__ than that!

how much better? your Chevy dealer can show you. . . . *Chevrolet Division of General Motors, Detroit 2, Michigan.*

Nearly all American cars adopted quad headlights for 1958, and the Corvette was no exception. In addition, pronounced "nostrils" flanked the grille, and faux louvers appeared between the hood's twin windsplits. The side coves sprouted fake scoops with horizontal chrome strakes, and taillights had a flush appearance thanks to clear red covers. Chrome trim strips on the decklid were a 1958-only design flourish. Save for the deletion of the hood louvers and trunklid chrome, the 1959 and '60 Vettes were visual carryovers, though the top fuel-injected engine was boosted to 315 hp for 1960. Advertising encouraged aspirational daydreaming, which must have helped: Corvette sales topped 10,000 units for the first time in 1960, the best sales year to date. The car's long-term future was now secure.

1961

twice a day he takes a vacation.

An all-new flowing "ducktail" rear end was the 1961 Corvette's biggest change. It added luggage space as well as visual appeal. Small round taillights sat alongside the central license-plate recess, while a modest creaseline extended through the trunklid's traditional round medallion. Simple bumperettes were mounted below the taillights, and the dual exhaust pipes now exited below the body. Body-color bezels helped clean up the quad-headlight nose, and the trademark grille teeth were removed and replaced with a horizontal mesh insert. For 1962, the side cove vents switched from chrome spears to simple vanes. And for the first time since their introduction on the '56 model, the coves couldn't wear a contrasting color.

1962

SOME GUYS HAVE IT
TOUGH

Corvette owners are not necessarily the most carefree people in the world, but there are moments when every Corvette driver must think himself thrice blest. Here's a car that, more than any other, has an uncanny ability to erase the day's cares and woes and whisk its driver far, far away. Turn on the key, engage first gear and step on it: Good-bye office, hello better things of life. We'll make no attempt to analyze the chemistry of such a phenomenon; it's all blurred by things like the feeling of wind on your face, the sound of the Corvette exhaust, the cyclone surge of a truly great V8 engine. We will be more than happy, however, to direct you to your nearest Chevrolet dealer to sample a Corvette. Look at it, sit in it, drive it, and you'll find that we haven't exaggerated a bit. We couldn't exaggerate these things if we tried. (Radio, as shown, optional at extra cost.) . . . Chevrolet Division of General Motors, Detroit 2, Michigan.

CORVETTE BY CHEVROLET

C2
1963-1967

With sales going nowhere but up, Chevrolet boldly ushered in a radically new Corvette that was again based on a show car, which itself was based on a racer. This dual parentage paid dividends in both styling and performance, and sales continued their upward trend. And with the muscle-car era in full swing, big-block power was added to the roster.

The Corvette Sting Ray bowed for 1963 with the previous year's engines in a stunning all-new package with a trimmer 98-inch wheelbase and first-time all-independent suspension. The trademark fiberglass body gained extra steel inner reinforcements and head-turning looks taken from Bill Mitchell's recent Stingray racer. The first production Corvette coupe also debuted, a sleek fastback with a distinctive split rear window. The coupe started at $4252, some $200 above the convertible, but buyers eagerly snapped up 10,594 for the model year. Some critics chided styling details like the simulated hood vents, but the Sting Ray design has come to be regarded as a modern classic.

1964

Just a minute! That's a '64 Corvette Sting Ray those two deserted to go perch on an everyday old rock and gaze at the piney woods! Ah well, love is seldom rational. Saner souls would harken to Corvette's windswept '64 styling, clean as the Sport Coupe's new one-piece rear window. They'd take to that dressed-up interior—new simulated walnut-rim steering wheel, new instrument faces, redesigned center console, an interior ventilator in Sport Coupe models to boost air circulation. People with both feet on the ground would hoist them aboard to sample Corvette's quieter, smoother ride; the muffled thunder of a V8 in one of four versions up to 375 hp*; or the joys of a new 4-speed manual transmission*, improved standard 3-speed or Powerglide automatic*. Clear thinkers know there are two Corvettes, the Sport Coupe above and the Convertible, plus a long list of comfort, convenience and performance options. No use telling all this to that Sweet Young Thing and her swain. Anyway, *you're* the one that we—and your Chevrolet dealer—are really interested in. . . . Chevrolet Division. of General Motors, Detroit, Michigan.   *OPTIONAL AT EXTRA COST

'64 CORVETTE STING RAY BY CHEVROLET

The Sting Ray entered 1964 with a few detail changes and the same base prices. The coupe now used a one-piece rear window for improved visibility, and the simulated hood vents were removed. The top-dog fuel-injected engine was now good for 375 horsepower, but few buyers were willing to fork over the $538 it added to the bottom line. Styling changes for 1965 were subtle but defining: The hood was devoid of '64's indents, and the twin side "scoops" behind the front wheels were traded for a trio of vertical vents. Mechanical changes included the welcome substitution of disc brakes for the previous drums, and the availability of big-block 396 V-8 power at midyear.

1965

The coupe will fill your life about as full as the convertible.
(Sorry, some decisions don't come easy.)

The Sting Ray Sport Coupe is a snug, cozy, intimate machine with plenty of luxurious room for two and their luggage. The Convertible is a snug, cozy, luxurious machine with plenty of luxurious room for two and their luggage, and the top goes down. Some people just like to be wind-blown every once in a while, and some don't.

You'll just have to make up your own mind. In either case you get all the benefits of Corvette ownership—things like four-wheel disc brakes. Four-wheel

independent suspension. 47/53 weight distribution. All-vinyl interior. Fiberglass body. That kind of thing.

And you get to make all the choices about what equipment you want to order for either car—like your choice of six engines and three transmissions, or such equipment as power windows, power steering, or power brakes. You'll get the same kind of handling, performance, and precision engineering in the coupe as you will in the convertible. Corvette-kind. Superb.

(If you absolutely can't make up your mind, you might consider both cars. You can buy them both for less than you'd have to pay for just one of a lot of other Grand Touring cars of similar performance and quality.)

Corvette Sting Ray

CHEVROLET

Chevrolet Division of General Motors, Detroit, Michigan

1966

Why men leave home.

No small wonder a man gets that faraway look—when there's a new Corvette in the driveway. After all, this is no ordinary car. This is a real out-and-out sports car with a new Turbo-Jet V8 you can order to make it go (up to 425 hp); 4-wheel disc brakes to make it stop; and an independent rear suspension to make it handle. This is a real, live Grand Touring machine that performs with the best in the world. Yet it's about as untemperamental as the family sedan. Corvette is a car designed for just one thing. It's to be driven—well and often, mind you—but driven. Let it sit idle on a Saturday afternoon, and you do it an injustice.

'66 CORVETTE BY CHEVROLET

Chevrolet Division of General Motors, Detroit, Michigan.

Chevy's new 427 big-block V-8 replaced the 396 as Corvette's top 1966 power option, offering 390 or 425 horsepower. Model-year production set another record with 17,762 ragtops and 9958 coupes. Bodies received another round of styling tweaks: a crosshatch-patterned grille replacing the previous horizontal bars; a Corvette script on the hood; and, for coupes, side roof pillars devoid of vents. Unusual "gold-line" tires were a $46.55 option. The year's most popular color was handsome Nassau Blue, which ended up on 6100 'Vettes. Zora Arkus-Duntov (pictured top left) could be justifiably proud, for the 'Vette's styling and performance had both been refined to near perfection.

1967

Several minor styling alterations marked the '67 Sting Ray. Five shorter front-fender gills replaced the former three, and, in the rear, a horizontal back-up light appeared over the license-plate frame. Big-block models got a revised hood scoop, and Rally wheels were newly available. Despite their exotic styling and extraordinary performance potential, Corvettes had become fairly practical and civilized beasts by 1967, thanks to available features such as leather upholstery, power windows, and air conditioning.

C3
1968-1982

As it turned out, Corvette's shortest-running generation would be followed by its longest. The C3 took Chevy's sports car through a tumultuous time in history, spanning the highs and lows of horsepower production and contending with a raft of new government regulations. Despite these challenges, the Corvette not only survived, but thrived.

The Oh-My-Heavens one. You release a few latches and those panels in the roof are ready for lift off. You release a few more and the rear window's ready for lift off. You flip the key in the ignition and you . . . and you . . . say, you're not listening. Hello, do you read us? What's the use. You're in a world all your own. **Corvette** Like a car, only better. CHEVROLET

10 seconds to lift off.

Sports Class winner of the Motor Trend 1968 Achievement Award, for which we thank them.

Originally planned for 1967 but delayed by development problems, the '68 Corvette wore a swoopy new body atop the 1963-67 chassis and dispensed with the Sting Ray name. Coupes got twin lift-off roof panels called "T-Tops," along with a removable rear window. The Sting Ray name went on hiatus for 1968 but returned as one word—Stingray—over the fender gills of 1969 'Vettes. Newly optional were side-mounted exhaust (after a year's absence) and chrome trim for the front-fender louvers. The '69 shown at left is one of only two aluminum big-block ZL-1 Corvettes sold to the public.

1970-1972

Trim changes, a bigger big-block, and flared wheel openings were the primary 'Vette updates for 1970. The 427 V-8 made way from the new 454, and a 370-hp LT1 350 was now the top small-block option. The '71s and '72s were virtually unchanged visually, but engines were detuned to run on the newly available unleaded fuel. The '72s were noteworthy for being the last 'Vettes to have chrome bumpers front and rear.

1973-1977

The role of the dream car in an age of reality.

Dreams.
They sustain us, they spur us. Sometimes they simply help soften the rough edges of our days.
In that noble regard, Corvette has performed with true distinction through the years.
To own such a fabled car as this one day, one time. Now that's a dream

that ranks with scaling tall mountains and sailing wide seas.
For most, for sure, it's a dream that remains unfulfilled. But remains, nonetheless.
Corvette, America's only true production sports car. With a shape and a stance and a spirit all its own. A classic

cockpit, disc brakes all around, fully independent suspension. And roof panels you can lift off to see the stars.
Our dream car is not without its practical aspects, of course. It has among other things a body that simply cannot corrode. (It's made of fiber glass.)

And there are just two seats. One for you, one for her. Does a dreamer need more?
Corvette. Not just a car, an inspiration.
Sweet dreams.

Chevrolet

For 1973, the 'Vette got a new front end that incorporated a urethane-covered bumper to meet the government's new five-mph front-impact regulations. It was joined by fenders with side scoops rather than the previous gills. A matching rear-end treatment was added for 1974 to meet the rear-impact standard enacted for that model year. This style would continue for many years, but the '74 version was unique in being molded in two pieces, with a "split" down the middle; later versions were one piece. The 1976 ad above hints at the somber times facing American automakers, but the 'Vette continued to sell well; output increased yearly from 30,464 in 1973 to 49,213 in 1977.

1978-1979

The biggest change to Corvette for 1978 was a "glassback" rear roofline that replaced the channeled buttresses used before. Not only did the new design provide better rear-corner visibility, it also allowed easier access to the cargo compartment. Inside, a three-spoke steering wheel was made standard, and a proper glovebox was added in place of the former vinyl map pocket. For '79, the front and rear spoilers first seen on the '78 Indy Pace Car became a $265 option which could only be ordered with the $380 aluminum wheels. Also, Corvette's base price topped $10K for the first time—$10,220.23, to be exact. Buyers didn't seem to mind; sales reached 53,807, a new record, and one that still stands.

1980-1982

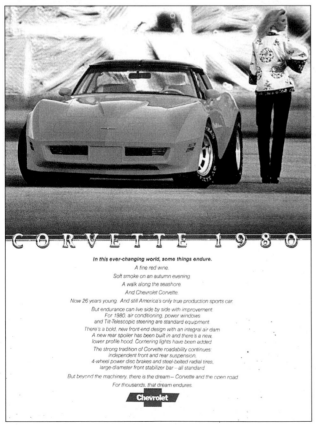

Corvettes received an effective facelift for 1980 that employed integrated front and rear spoilers, revised front fender vents, and a new crossed-flag nose emblem. The top engine choice for '80 was an L82 350 V-8 that made 230 horsepower, but California buyers had to make do with a 180-hp 305 V-8 due to stricter emissions in that state. The 1981 Corvettes were built in two plants as production shifted from the St. Louis factory to a new facility in Bowling Green, Kentucky. Engine choices were dropped to just one for '81: a 190-hp L83 350 V-8. Ever-tightening emissions standards were challenging engineers, and for 1982, Corvette adopted Cross-Fire Injection to become the first "fuelie" 'Vette since 1965. The four-speed manual transmission was dropped, meaning that for the first time since 1954, all Corvettes came with an automatic. The two-tone paint seen on the 1982 'Vette at bottom right was a $428 option.

C4
1984-1996

Few cars have been more fervently rumored and eagerly anticipated than the fourth-generation Corvette. Skipping the 1983 model year—and thus its 30th anniversary—the C4 was introduced to great fanfare and glowing accolades as a 1984 model. It signaled a turnaround in the Corvette's mission, once again stressing "sport" over "luxury." Plus, horsepower was on the rise again, culminating with the mighty ZR-1.

Despite an entirely new look, the C4 was instantly recognizable as a Corvette, having retained such features as round taillights and a chiseled, tapered snout. If somewhat less "sexy" than the curvaceous C3, the taut surfaces of the C4 lent it a more purposeful look and yielded improved aerodynamics. Practicality was obviously given consideration in the design. The flip-up rear glass opened to a large cargo well between the seats and the fuel tank, and a forward-tilting clamshell hood granted access to the entire front end of the car. The roof was removable, as in the C3, but the opening was devoid of the T-top's center bar. The Cross-Fire Injection 5.7-liter V-8 carried over from 1982, but now with 205 hp versus 200, and it came standard with a four-speed automatic transmission. A four-speed manual returned as a no-cost option.

1985-1988

The 1985 Corvette priced about $1500 higher than the already-steep $23,360 base price of the '84, but the extra money bought 25 extra horsepower, thanks to a switch from throttle-body fuel injection to the more-efficient multiport type. Chevy called its system "Tuned Port Injection," which appeared on discreet front fender badges to signal the change. And, after more than a decade without one, the Corvette got a convertible variant for 1986. For 1987, the horsepower rating inched up to 240, thanks to roller rocker arms and 1986's aluminum heads, which were now standard. New six-slot 16-inch wheels were standard for 1988.

1989-1990

C4 convertibles finally got an optional hard-top in 1989. It could be retrofitted to earlier versions, and it's seen opposite being placed on an '86. Seventeen-inch wheels were now standard, and the optional manual transmission was now a six-speed. In 1989, Chevy first showed the new ultra-performance ZR-1 model, which packed a dual-overhead-cam 5.7-liter V-8 that made 375 hp. External differences were limited to wider rear flanks (to cover massive 11-inch-wide rear tires), a convex rear fascia, squarish taillights, and subtle badges. ZR-1s were assembled alongside regular Corvettes, but their Lotus-designed aluminum V-8s came from a Mercury Marine plant in Oklahoma. Though originally planned for 1989, production ZR-1s didn't arrive until the '90 model year.

1991-1996

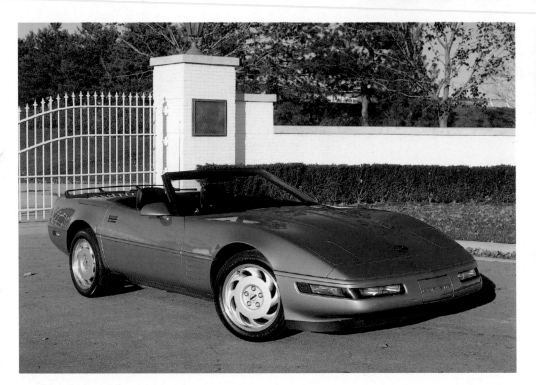

A 1991 facelift brought a more rounded nose, revised front-fender vents, and a ZR-1-style rear fascia to all Corvettes. Save for restyled fender gills for 1995, the basic styling would remain essentially unchanged for the remainder of the C4's run. For 1992, base 'Vettes got a gutsy new LT1 V-8 that put out 300 hp, 50 more than the L98 it replaced. ZR-1 sales dropped as the substantially cheaper base Corvette matched its styling and came closer to matching its horsepower. Despite a 30-hp bump to 405 hp for 1993, ZR-1 demand dwindled, and the model was dropped after 1995. For 1996, a new 330-hp LT4 engine was fitted to six-speed 'Vettes, while automatics kept the 300-hp LT1.

C5
1997-2004

With the C4 growing long in the tooth from its 13-year run, Chevrolet brought forth a curvaceous, state-of-the-art successor that maintained the Corvette heritage while upping the ante in the sports-car sweepstakes. Both the automotive press and the public raved; the C5 exhibited a level of style, sophistication, and outright performance that awed longtime fans and attracted new ones.

Hailed as the best Corvette yet, the all-new 1997 C5 put a slinky new body on a new more rigid perimeter frame. It was birthed by Dave Hill (pictured top right), who took over from Dave McClellan as the new-model program got under way. The C5's wheelbase grew a massive 8.3 inches to 104.5, the longest in 'Vette history, and length was up by 1.2 inches, yet base curb weight actually fell by some 80 pounds. A 5.7-liter pushrod V-8 remained the only powerplant for the C5, but it too was all-new like the rest of the car. With 345 hp, it was more potent than even the short-lived LT4. With standard six-speed manual shift, the new 'Vette vaulted from 0-60 mph in just under 5 seconds. A hatchback coupe was the only model for '97; after a one-year hiatus, a convertible returned to the lineup for 1998. It was the first Corvette ragtop since 1962 to have a trunklid for easier cargo access. Even better, it was almost as rigid as the hatchback and no less quick, as it weighed virtually the same. *Motor Trend* magazine was suitably impressed, honoring Corvette as its 1998 Car of the Year.

1999-2000

While 1999 brought few changes for the carryover coupe and convertible, it brought big news in the form of a new model. Dubbed "hardtop" by Chevy, the new notchback 'Vette featured a solid one-piece roof instead of the removable panel found on the coupe. The simpler construction offered greater structural rigidity—though Corvette was already earning praise for its stout construction—and a modest 92-pound weight reduction. Intended to be a serious sports car, the hardtop came standard with the six-speed manual transmission and Z51 performance suspension, options which totaled $1195 on a coupe or convertible. New slim-spoke wheels debuted for 2000 along with Millennium Yellow paint, an eye-grabbing color than cost $500 extra. Despite its lower price, the hardtop's sales trailed far behind the coupe and convertible: just 2090 were built for 2000, versus 18,113 coupes and 13,479 convertibles.

2001

For 2001, the slow-selling hardtop was transformed into the Z06, the highest-horsepower Corvette since the ZR-1. The new Z06 wore unique mesh grille inserts, rear brake cooling ducts, wider new-design wheels, and specially developed Goodyear Eagle F1 SC tires. A beefier clutch and a revised six-speed manual transaxle helped deliver the extra power provided by a new LS6 version of the aluminum V-8. This Z06-exclusive engine was rated at 385 hp. Result: the fastest production Corvette yet, besting even the storied ZR-1. Meanwhile, the base Corvettes were visually unchanged but received several incremental improvements, including a 5-horsepower bump to 350 total.

Z06

Some will say it's overkill. The way we've obsessed over making Z06™ lighter and more rigid. They'll say a titanium exhaust that shaves 17 pounds is excessive. That shot-peening the rear axle's ring gear to handle more torque is too much. And thinning the windshield to reduce 2.2 pounds? Over the line. Well, the Z06 goes 0 to 60 in 4 seconds and handles 1 g of lateral acceleration. So be sure to wave at those people as you pass them on the track. CorvetteZ06.com

Corvette is a registered trademark of the GM Corp. ©2000 GM Corp. Buckle up, America! ☎1-800-950-2438

INTRODUCING AN ENTIRELY NEW LEVEL OF *OVERKILL.*

2002-2004

The C5 Corvette saw no major revisions from 2002 to 2004, but it did get a number of enticing enhancements. For its sophomore season, Z06 got even hotter thanks to a 20-hp boost, to 405. Chevy claimed the Z06 could run 0-60 in just 3.9 seconds and complete a quarter-mile sprint in a mere 12.4 seconds at 114 mph. For 2003, a sophisticated new Magnetic Selective Ride Control suspension became available as a $1695 option. The system used magnetically charged fluid to constantly adjust shock-absorber firmness based on road conditions and driving style. The bodyside moldings shown on the silver 2003 Z06 and 2004 coupe on this page were a $75 option that helped protect against dings and dents.

C6
2005-

With the C6 generation, Chevrolet built on the already impressive C5 by giving it tidier dimensions, more horsepower, and less weight—a surefire formula for greater performance. And perform it did, even before the advent of the revived Z06 and ZR1, both of which set standards that few cars in the world could match.

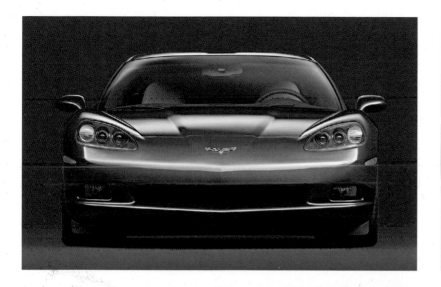

More an evolution of the C5 than an all-new car, the 2005 Corvette C6 took giant steps forward in performance and refinement. Designers abandoned the hideaway headlamps that had been a Corvette staple since 1963, but some classic Sting Ray influence was visible in the peaked fender shapes. Under the hood was a 400-hp 6.0-liter LS2 engine—a bored-out version of the LS1 that debuted in the 1997 Corvette. Unlike the C4 and C5 'Vettes, the C6 offered a convertible right from the start. It started at $52,245, a significant premium over the $43,710 base price of the coupe. The C5's hardtop body style was discontinued. Not surprisingly, the dazzling C6 was well received, and production rose almost ten percent, to 37,372 units..

2006

Chevrolet revived the Z06 model on the C6 platform for 2006. The new Z06 could be distinguished by its nose-mounted air intake and rear brake cooling scoops (which were shared with the C6.R race car), fixed roof, flared fenders, and unique wheels on monster 18-inch front and 19-inch rear tires. The Z06's 7.0-liter LS7 V-8 put out a whopping 505 hp and 470 lb-ft of torque; *Car and Driver* took its test Z06 to a blistering 3.6-second 0-60 time and a 11.7-second quarter mile. NASCAR superstar Jeff Gordon (left) appeared on a episode of SPEED Channel's *Test Drive* program in fall 2005, piloting the new Z06 on the Road Atlanta race course with show host Tommy Kendall (right).

2007-2008

Corvettes were mostly unchanged for 2007, though vibrant new Atomic Orange Tintcoat Metallic paint (shown below) replaced Daytona Sunset Orange on the color palette. For 2008, a new 6.2-liter LS3 V-8 with 430 hp replaced the 400-hp LS2. An optional dual-mode exhaust system used vacuum-actuated outlet valves that minimized noise when cruising, but opened for maximum performance in heavy-throttle operation. The system boosted peak hp to 436 and had the added benefit of a more-aggressive exhaust note. Also new for '08 were wheels with slightly slimmer, less-angular spokes. By any measure, 'Vette performance was better than ever—even a base model with automatic transmission was capable of a 4.3-second 0-60-mph time, and the mighty Z06 continued to reign. Still, the rumor mill was buzzing that an even-more-potent über-'Vette would debut soon.

2009

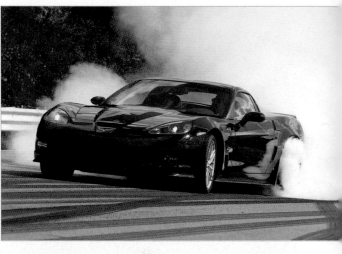

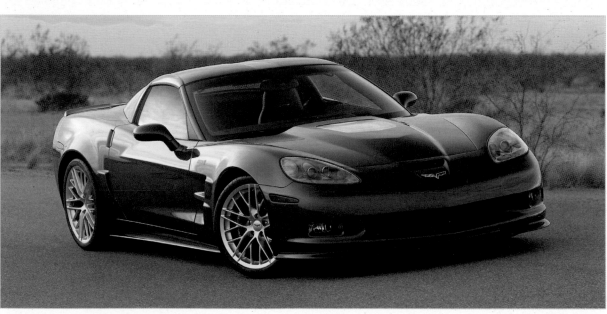

The much-rumored über-'Vette turned out to be the 2009 ZR1, and it was a jaw-dropper indeed: 638 horsepower, 604 lb-ft of torque, 0-60 mph in less than 3.5 seconds, and a 205-mph top speed. A supercharged "LS9" version of the 6.2-liter V-8 provided the outstanding power. Gigantic carbon-ceramic brake rotors and lightweight carbon-fiber body panels were among the many exotic components. Some testing and development occurred at Germany's famed Nürburgring road course (opposite, bottom right). The $103,970 base price was certainly sobering, but considering that the ZR1 could outperform most any high-dollar European supercar, it was still something of a bargain.

2010

Base Corvettes, ZR1s, and Z06s (all opposite) were mostly unchanged for 2010, but the model lineup expanded to include new Grand Sport coupes and convertibles (this page). Reviving the name of the famous early-Sixties 'Vette race car (and the 1996 limited-edition models), Grand Sport essentially bridged the performance and appearance gap between a base 2010 Corvette and the Z06; its LS2 engine was shared with the base Corvette, but it inherited some of the Z06's body and suspension upgrades. Exclusive trim features such as the front-fender "gills" and driver-side hash-mark stripes gave the Grand Sport its own unique character. A Grand Sport coupe started at $54,770—about $6000 more than a base coupe, but almost $20K cheaper than a Z06.

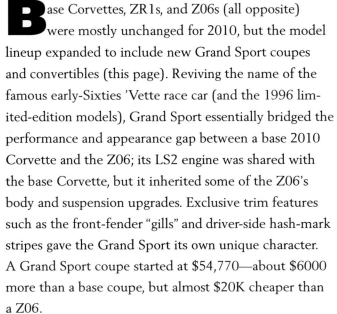

CHAPTER TWO

Wheels of Progress

A flashy car like the Corvette needs "footwear" to match. Chevrolet designers always made sure that the 'Vette rolled on eye-catching wheel-and-tire combos that kept pace with the latest in performance-car technology—and projected a high-style image. Over the years, the 'Vette's various hubcaps and wheels have become icons in and of themselves.

Below: *Early production 1953 Corvettes made do with standard-Chevy wheelcovers (left); flashier Corvette-exclusive units (right) arrived shortly.*

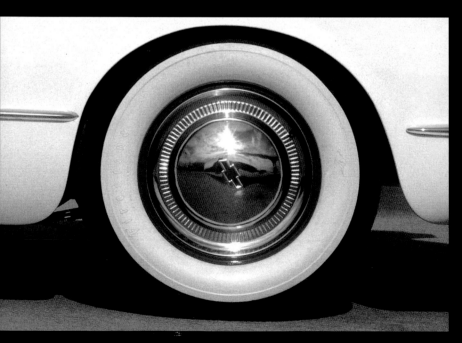

Not all early 'Vettes wore fancy wheel-covers and whitewalls; this all-business '57 sports base-model Chevy hubcaps.

The 1958 Corvette hubcap was basically unchanged from 1956/57. Simulated "knock-off" spinners looked great in motion.

The 1959 Corvette could also get the "no-frills" treatment via mainstream Chevy "dog-dish" hubcaps. Hardcore enthusiasts appreciated this bare-bones look.

Above: *'Vette hubcaps gained rectangular slots for '59, and narrow whitewall tires debuted for '62.* **Left:** *Handsome cast-aluminum wheels with tri-spinner knock-offs debuted with the dazzling 1963 Sting Ray.*

Left: *Nineteen-sixty-three Sting Ray buyers who didn't want to spring for the extra-cost aluminum wheels got these attractive hubcaps with faux knock-off spinners.* **Above:** *Revised hubcaps with a smoother, more simplified design were one of the many detail changes on the 1964 Sting Rays.*

Top and above: *Hubcap designs were revised again for '65 (top) and '66 (above). The '66 design vaguely mimicked the look of the popular aftermarket "mag" wheels of the era.*

Above: *For 1967, the Corvette's cast-aluminum wheel design was revised to include a screw-off center cap that covered traditional lug nuts.* **Right:** *Chevrolet's popular (and prolific) five-hole "Rally" wheels also debuted for '67, along with redline tires.*

Above: *Full-face wheelcovers with a "turbine" motif debuted for 1968. This design was shared with other Chevrolet passenger cars, but only Corvettes got the crossed-flags center cap.*

Left and above: *The Rally wheel got new center caps for '68, and would remain available on Corvettes until 1982. Other Chevrolet cars used Rally wheels too, but only 'Vettes wore these extra-wide versions with "deep-dish" trim rings.*

Left: *Slotted aluminum wheels first appeared on the options list for 1973, but manufacturing problems delayed their general release until '76.* **Above:** *The '78 Indy Pace Car wheels got a polish and a red pinstripe.*

The 1982 Collector Edition Corvette wore exclusive aluminum wheels that recalled the classic "turbine" wheels of the original Sting Rays. Outline white-letter tires were new for '78.

The redesigned 1984 Corvette took a big leap forward in wheel-and-tire technology: wide 16-inch alloy wheels on low-profile Goodyear "gatorback" rubber designed specifically for the 'Vette.

Seventeen-inch wheels became available on 'Vettes for 1988 as part of a performance handling package. For 1989, these new wheels were made standard across the board.

For 1990, the basic 17-inch wheel from 1988 and '89 was revised; the detachable center cap was deleted, and the bolt circle was now exposed.

A new wheel design debuted for 1991 to complement the minor facelift that all Corvettes received that year.

ZR-1s for 1994 got five-spoke wheels that weren't offered on base Corvettes.

The limited-edition 1996 Grand Sports got five-spoke wheels finished in black with a silver rim lip as one of their exclusive features.

New "C5" Corvettes debuted for 1997, and boasted new wheels with staggered sizing: 17 inches in the front, and 18 in the rear.

The '98 Indy Pace Car wore the same wheels as other C5 'Vettes, but dressed them in an eye-searing yellow hue.

A new five-spoke wheel design with slimmer spokes debuted for 2000. Both polished (shown) and satin finishes were available.

The extreme-performance Z06 debuted for 2001 wearing unique, extra-wide wheels on specially developed Goodyear F1 SC tires. The wheels' open design provided a nice view of the Z06's massive drilled brake rotors and red calipers.

Above: *The C6 Corvette was unleashed for 2005 wearing new five-spoke wheels that measured 18 inches up front and 19 out back. 'Vettes equipped with the Z51 Performance Handling Package got drilled brake rotors.* **Right:** *The new-for-2006 Z06 wore this exclusive wheel design.*

Above: *The awe-inspiring 2009 ZR1 wore staggered 19/20-inch wheels on massive Michelin rubber.* **Below:** *Z06s were treated to a new wheel design for 2009.*

Left: *The 2010 Corvette Grand Sport wore these unique thin-spoke wheels. The polished chrome finish seen here was an extra-cost option.* **Right:** *The 2011 Z06 Carbon Edition gained some of the top-dog ZR1 Corvette's enhancements, including Brembo carbon-ceramic brakes and black-finished versions of the ZR1's 20-inch wheels— complete with a "Z06 Carbon" insignia on the rim.*

CHAPTER THREE

Show Cars, Concepts, and One-Offs

The very first Corvette debuted to wide-eyed adulation as a glamorous show car, so it's only natural that concept vehicles and one-off dream machines have long been a key part of the 'Vette's allure. Over the years, these remarkable automobiles have included GM's "official" Corvette show machines; rebodied specials crafted by European coachbuilders; and one-of-a-kind customs built for celebrities, GM executives, and other VIPs. Part of the reason these cars are so enticing is that their special design and engineering features often trickle down to the Corvettes that the general public can buy at their Chevrolet dealership. That original 1953 Motorama Corvette show car turned out to be a near-exact match to the production 'Vette that graced showrooms not long after. Time will tell if tomorrow's production Corvettes reflect the groundbreaking styling of the 2009 Stingray Concept.

The 2009 Stingray Concept was the first full-blown Corvette concept vehicle in well over a decade. Though it lifted some design themes from the classic 1963 Sting Ray, the overall look was thoroughly futuristic.

1953 Motorama Show Car

Chevrolet unveiled the first Corvette in January 1953 at General Motors's first Motorama show of the year, held at New York City's Waldorf-Astoria hotel. An enthusiastic reception convinced GM brass to put the flashy two-seater into production, which commenced some six months later. The original show car differed only in detail from its production kin; its unique features included thinner headlight bezels, fender-top scoops, and abbreviated bodyside chrome trim. For the 1954 Motorama shows, Chevrolet cooked up three Corvette concepts (opposite page): a mostly-stock 'Vette with a removable hardtop (a feature that would soon see production), a rakish Nomad station wagon, and a fastback coupe dubbed the Corvair (seen here in both light and dark paint colors).

1954 Motorama Show Cars

1950s Ghia-bodied Coupe

It didn't take long for the stylish Corvette to attract the attention of customizers and coachbuilding firms. This one-of-a-kind Ferrari-esque coupe combines a 1954 Corvette chassis and powertrain with aluminum bodywork constructed by Ghia Aigle of Switzerland, an affiliate of Italy's famed Ghia coachworks. Built for the 1957 Geneva Auto Show, it was designed by Giovanni Michelotti, who later penned several sports cars for Triumph in England. GM's own designers and engineers also loved tinkering with Corvettes; this September 1956 "family portrait" photo (opposite) shows Chevy's SR-2 Corvette concept/race cars surrounded by a variety of one-off modified Corvettes. The 1957 Super Sport show car (opposite, bottom) sported a unique "double-bubble" windscreen, broad dorsal racing stripes, and forward-facing scoops built into the aft portions of the bodyside coves.

GM Design Cars/1957 Super Sport

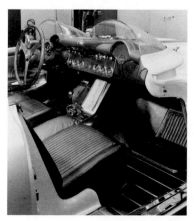

1958-60 XP-700

1961 Mako Shark

Bill Mitchell succeeded Harley Earl as GM's design chief in late 1958, and the 1958-60 XP-700 show car was designed and built under his supervision. The XP-700's copious body scoops, oval-shaped snout, sunken headlights, side pipes, and clear "bubble" top were fanciful features that wouldn't see the showroom floor, but its "ducktail" rear end would appear on production Corvettes for 1961. The 1961 Mako Shark reflected Mitchell's interest in sharks as a design inspiration (note the tacked-up shark pictures in the design rendering photo above). Its sharp, sharklike nose—complete with gill-like scoops—gave the Mako Shark an aggressive look that would influence the production 1963 Sting Ray. Both the XP-700 and Mako Shark are shown here with Mitchell and the 1959 Stingray show/race cars. The color photo of the Mako Shark at right depicts a later version with a darker paint job, cast-aluminum wheels, and other styling updates.

Four-seat Mock-up/
1964 NY World's Fair Show Car

Chevrolet briefly considered a four-seat Sting Ray "2+2" coupe at the urging of division chief Ed Cole. The idea got as far as a full-size mock-up, shown above alongside a rival Ford Thunderbird. The 1964 New York World's Fair Sting Ray show car (right) featured several unique styling details, among them an eggcrate-pattern grille, wild side pipes, and a raised fuel-injection unit that protruded though a hole in the hood. GM styling chief Bill Mitchell customized a new 1963 Sting Ray convertible (opposite) as a gift to his predecessor, Harley Earl. Features included a leather-lined cockpit with extra gauges, a hopped-up 327 with side exhaust, and racing stripes.

1963 Harley Earl Convertible

1965 Mako Shark II

Mako Shark II/Manta Ray

The 1965 Mako Shark II concept car previewed 1968 production Corvette styling. There were actually two Mako Shark IIs built; the original (shown above) debuted at the New York Auto Show and was a nonrunning vehicle with side exhaust pipes. A second, fully functional Mako Shark II debuted later in 1965 at the Paris Auto Salon; it's shown opposite with Bill Mitchell and the original 1961 Mako Shark show car. Chevy's new 427-cubic-inch V-8 lurked under the "II"'s hood, and its far-out show-car features included front parking lights hidden behind power-retractable "gills," and a pop-up roof panel for easier entry and exit. The seats were fixed, but the gas and brake pedals were adjustable to accommodate different-sized drivers. The Mako Shark II was updated in 1969 to become the Manta Ray (right). A restyled roofline, chin spoiler, and Chevy's exotic new all-aluminum 427-cid ZL-1 V-8 were among the additions.

1968 Astro-Vette/Astro II

1969 Aero Coupe/1970 Scirocco

The 1968 Astro-Vette concept (opposite top) was based on a production '68 Corvette convertible, but was revamped by GM stylists to include a cut-down wraparound windscreen, targa bar, faux front-fender side flaps, and top-hinged rear wheel skirts. The monochromatic front bumper and convex rear body shape eventually made it into production. Though it wasn't officially a Corvette, the 1968 XP-880 Astro II (opposite bottom) stoked enthusiast dreams of a mid-engined 'Vette. It wouldn't be the last time Chevrolet flirted with the idea. The 1969 Aero Coupe show car (top) featured an integral rear spoiler and a single lift-off roof panel instead of a T-roof. "Cheese grater" front fender vents forecast a 1970 change. Soon, the Aero Coupe received a minor redo that included a body-color front bumper, high-mounted rearview mirrors, an arrow-shaped hood/nose bulge, and a roof fairing that housed a rearview TV camera. Pinstripe body graphics added further pizzazz. In this form, it was renamed Scirocco.

1970 XP-882/1973 AeroVette

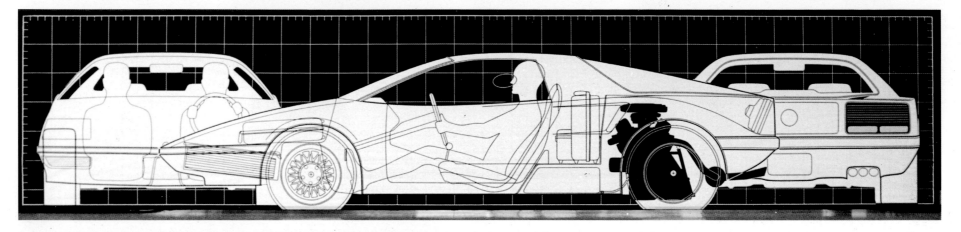

GM continued to toy with the idea of a mid-engined Corvette throughout the Seventies. The XP-882 (left) was revealed in 1970, while the design sketch (above) dates from 1975. The XP-882 soon begat another 'Vette concept (bottom and opposite) that originally appeared in 1973. This car was initially referred to as the 4-Rotor because of its unusual power source: two joined Wankel rotary engines that produced 420 hp and could push the car to a reported 145 mph. However, fuel economy concerns were the downfall of this exotic experimental powerplant. After the rotary engine was removed and replaced with a 454 V-8, the car was renamed AeroVette and did another tour of the auto-show circuit. Many thought the AeroVette was a preview of the next-generation showroom 'Vette, and it did come close to reaching production for 1980.

1973 AeroVette

1974 Mulsanne

Chevrolet usually got good mileage out of its Corvette show cars. The 1974 Mulsanne show car seen on this page is in fact a revamped version of the Aero Coupe/Scirocco that was first unveiled in 1969. In addition to the 1974-style front and rear fascias, the Mulsanne featured fixed rectangular headlamps behind clear plastic covers, side pipes, and the attractive Chaparral "lace" alloy wheels that appeared on several GM concepts of the day. Chevy also teased the public with several experimental turbocharged Corvettes. Shown clockwise from top left on the opposite page are the turbo Corvette concepts from 1978, '79, and '81, respectively. Chevrolet's 350-cubic-inch V-8 was muscled up with a Garrett turbocharger and a new type of GM fuel injection. Horsepower was in the neighborhood of 300—an impressive number when stock 'Vettes were making 180-230 hp.

Turbo Corvette Concepts

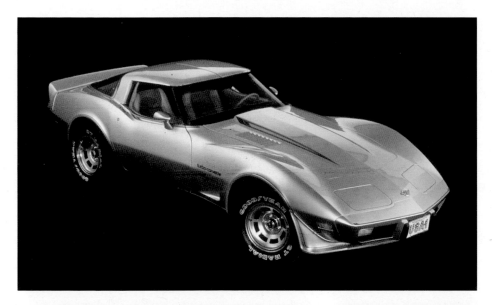

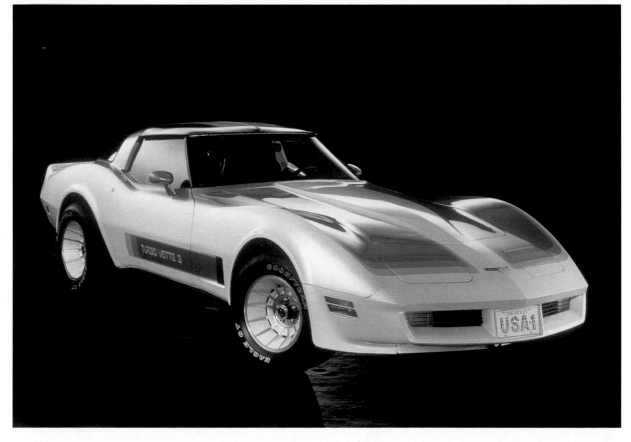

1985 Ramarro/1986 Corvette Indy

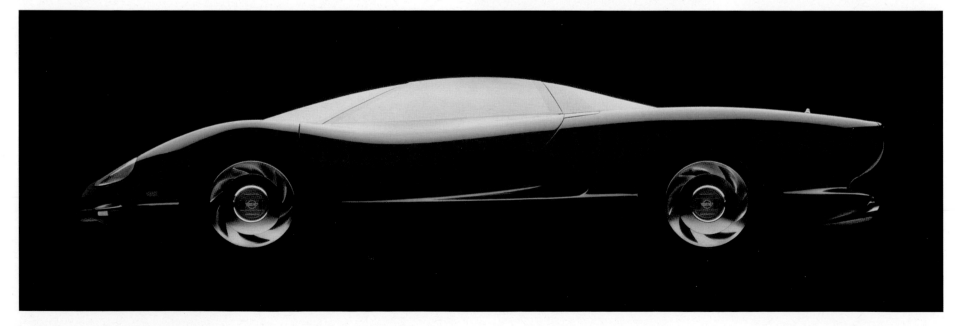

Corvette Indy/1990 CERV III

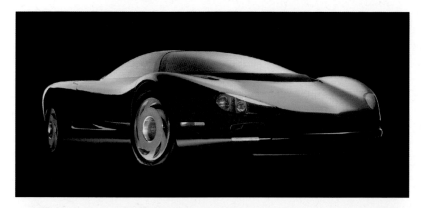

The craftsmen at Italy's famed Carozzeria Bertone design studio created the radical Ramarro (opposite, top left) from a 1984 Corvette chassis for the 1985 European auto-show season. Hard-edged body styling is evident in this profile view. Meanwhile in Detroit, the 1986 Corvette Indy concept showed that dreams of mid-engined Corvettes were still alive. The red car shown here is a functional vehicle; the silver car shown above is a nonrunning "pushmobile." The Indy's advanced features included all-wheel drive, four-wheel steering, and a body made mostly of carbon fiber. Pictured on this page at upper right are (L to R) Dave Hill, Zora Arkus-Duntov, and Dave McClellan—three generations of Corvette engineering chiefs. The 1990 CERV III concept (right) built on the design themes of the Indy concept and was powered by a twin-turbocharged 650-hp 5.7-liter V-8 mounted amidships.

1992 Stingray III

The 1992 Stingray III concept was designed at GM's Advanced Concept Center in Southern California. Its swoopy, organic body shapes didn't directly influence the styling direction of later production 'Vettes, though elements of its design did show up on future GM cars. Under the hood was a 300-hp LT-1 V-8 connected to a rear-mounted transaxle. A pop-up rollbar was a novel safety feature that later showed up on some production European-brand convertibles. The White Shark (opposite bottom), shown at the 2002 SEMA (Specialty Equipment Market Association) show in Las Vegas, was a modified production Corvette hardtop that packed a 6.6-liter V-8 with 512 horsepower and 523 lb-ft. of torque. Custom body touches included special front and rear fascias, a bulged hood, and tri-stage "Shark Sand" pearl paint.

Stingray III/2002 White Shark

2007 C6RS

Talk-show funnyman and "car guy" Jay Leno teamed up with Pratt and Miller, the engineering company responsible for Chevy's C6.R Corvette race cars, to create the C6RS. This wild one-off 'Vette debuted at the 2007 SEMA show. Performance and appearance enhancements abounded, and the C6RS's 600-hp 7.0-liter V-8 was designed to run on E85 ethanol fuel. The radical Stingray Concept was unveiled at the 2009 Chicago Auto Show, and also had a starring role in that year's summer blockbuster *Transformers II: Revenge of the Fallen*. Chevrolet billed the 2009 Stingray as a 50th anniversary tribute to the original 1959 race car.

2009 Stingray Concept

Skin Deep

Image has always been as important to the Corvette mystique as performance. It's doubtful the Corvette would have captured the imaginations of so many if it was merely a fast, great handling car. What's more, the Corvette's head-turning looks helped it maintain dream-car status even when its performance was decidedly less than neck-snapping.

Below: *High-mounted "rocket-pod" taillights adorned with tiny angled fins graced 1953-'55 'Vettes, along with racy inset headlights under screen-mesh covers.*

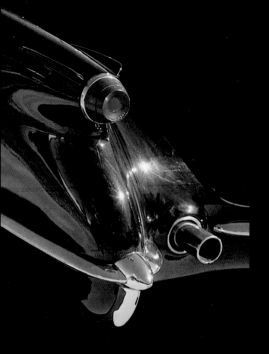

Left: *Exhaust pipes that exited through the body were an early 'Vette feature. The '54s wore longer tips to avoid the paint discoloration caused by the '53's pipes.* **Above:** *A stylish chrome bar with 13 "teeth" filled the grille opening of 1953-'57 'Vettes.* **Right:** *For 1956, Corvettes got more-rounded rear fenders with slick inset taillights.*

Right: *Corvette's handsome bodyside coves were dressed up for 1958 with faux side scoops dressed with chrome strakes. As in 1956-'57, the coves could be finished in a contrasting color for an extra fee.*

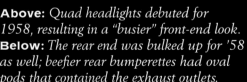

Above: *Quad headlights debuted for 1958, resulting in a "busier" front-end look.* **Below:** *The rear end was bulked up for '58 as well; beefier rear bumperettes had oval pods that contained the exhaust outlets.*

Left: *An upswept "ducktail" rear end with inset round taillights and license-plate cove debuted for 1961. The look hinted at the all-new styling of the 1963 Sting Ray.* **Above:** *For '62, side coves were shorn of their chrome bordering and updated with revised scoop trim.*

Left: *The hideaway headlights introduced on the 1963 Sting Ray would be a Corvette design staple for more than 40 years.* **Below:** *Simulated hood-vent panels were a 1963-only Sting Ray design flourish.*

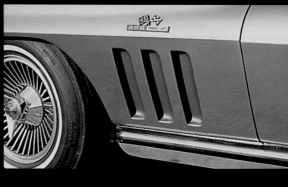

Above: *The 1963 Sting Ray's split rear window was a source of friction between Bill Mitchell and Zora Arkus-Duntov. Mitchell insisted it was an integral part of the design; Duntov hated the compromised rear visibility. Mitchell won for '63, but for '64 the split was removed.*

Above: *For 1965, the Sting Ray's front-fender louvers became three functional vertical slots.* **Right:** *Handsome inset taillights remained unchanged from 1963 to 1967.*

Below: *A spring-loaded finger plate with a separate door-latch button was a 1968-only feature. For '69, the latch mechanism was designed into the finger plate.*

Above: *An aggressive-looking "stinger" hood scoop was exclusive to 1967 big-block 'Vettes.* **Left:** *A new "power bulge" hood design debuted on the 1968 big-block 'Vettes.*

Above: *The '68 'Vette's radical new shape featured a slightly concave rear fascia and "tunnelback" rear roof styling. The signature dual round taillights were retained. There was still no externally accessible trunk space, but an add-on luggage rack could offer a bit of cargo capacity.*

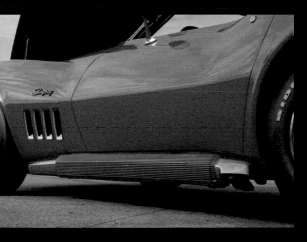

Racy-looking side pipes were optional from 1965 to '67 and returned for 1969 only as a $147.45 option. In place of the slotted heat shields of the 1965-'67 design, the '69 pipes wore thin horizontal ribs.

Tinkering with front-fender vent designs was a simple way for GM stylists to keep the basic Corvette shape looking fresh. For 1970, the vertical fender slots gave way to more-elaborate "cheese grater" vents.

The most striking change made to the 1973 Corvette was its body color beak. The new nose hid a stouter bumper that complied with government-ordered impact standards.

Above: *Front fender vents became simple scoops for 1973 and continued unchanged until 1979. The Stingray badge appeared for the last time on the 1976 models.* **Above right:** *The tunnelback roof's swan song season was 1977.* **Right:** *A facelift for 1980 brought a new rear fascia with an integral rear spoiler.*

Right: *Also part of the 1980 facelift were restyled side scoops. Flared fender openings helped protect the body sides from rock chips.*

Left: *Instead of the "pop-up" headlights of the 1968-'82 Corvette, the 1984 C4's headlights rotated at their midpoint for a slightly sleeker "exposed" appearance. A single square headlamp replaced two round lenses.* **Above:** *Like the rest of the C4 body, the front fender vents became more angular. The clamshell hood's break line was cleverly hidden by the black bodyside molding.*

Left: *The 1990 ZR-1's squarish taillights and convex rear fascia were passed on to other 'Vettes for 1991.* **Below:** *Also for 1991, front fender vents wore horizontal strakes instead of vertical gills.*

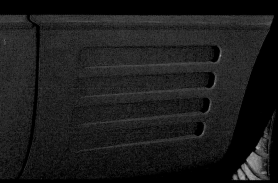

Left: *The 1997 C5 Corvette was much more rounded and "sculpted" than the car it replaced. The front-fender scoop's crease line now extended into the door.* **Above:** *C5 'Vettes offered small fog lamps as a $69 option. They nestled neatly within the front fascia's air intakes. Note the black air dam peeking out from underneath the nose.*

Above: *The C5 Corvette's removable roof panel stowed neatly in the rear cargo area for open-air motoring.* **Below:** *The 2006 Z06 sported beefier front-fender vents with Z06 badges.*

Above: *Front fender scoops became angular and more-pronounced with the debut of the new 2005 C5 'Vette.* **Right:** *Also for '05, designers abandoned the 'Vette's trademark hidden head-lamps in favor of lighter-weight exposed units.*

Left: *The 2009 Corvette ZR1 boasted lots of exclusive styling details. Perhaps the most intriguing was a unique bulged hood with a polycarbonate window that showed off the supercharged engine's inter-cooler.* **Right:** *The 2010 Grand Sport's front fenders were wider than the base 'Vette's. Functional fender vents had an aggressive "twin gill" design topped with chrome Grand Sport badges—just the ticket for extra cruise-night cred.*

CHAPTER FIVE

Race Cars

Despite their head-turning looks, the first Corvettes were no prize in the performance department. And after dismal sales early on, GM upper management was on the verge of dropping the car entirely. Salvation came from engineer Zora Arkus-Duntov, who wanted Chevrolet to be a key player in the fast-growing world of sports-car racing, and from Chevy's fabulous new small-block V-8. As the 1950s progressed, Duntov and his team worked tirelessly to transform the Corvette from boulevard cruiser to true sports-car superstar, and the lessons learned on the track were transferred to future production 'Vettes. Competition essentially saved the fledgling Corvette's life, and has been an indispensable part of its DNA ever since. With the advent of the C5-R and C6.R racing programs, Chevrolet has clearly demonstrated that it continues to value the link between racing Corvettes and their showroom kin.

Fifty years of Corvette racing history in one photo: A 2005 Corvette C6.R and a 1956 Corvette Sebring racer pose at the start/finish line of the famed Sebring International Raceway.

Early Racing Corvettes

1956 SR-2

The Corvette's competition history got rolling in 1955, with the arrival of the soon-to-be-legendary small-block V-8 engine. Scenes from these early exploits include (opposite, counterclockwise from top) a 1955 Corvette at the Pure Oil Trials at Daytona Beach, Florida; Zora Arkus-Duntov wheeling a '56 at Daytona Beach; a '57 racer undergoing a trackside refuel; and a '56 in action at an SCCA production-car race at Pebble Beach, California. Chevrolet started getting serious about racing the Corvette with the SR-2. The original SR-2 was built in March 1956 for Harley Earl's son Jerry, who raced the car at various tracks. Though clearly based on the production 1956 Corvette, the SR-2 had a reshaped nose with integrated foglamps, bodyside scoops, a double-bubble windscreen, and a trunk-mounted fin. Taking the wheel in the photo at right is Ed Cole, then Chevrolet's chief engineer.

1956-1957 SR-2

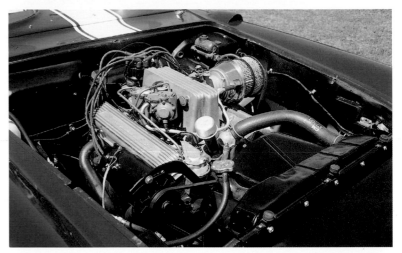

Bill Mitchell, who would soon succeed Harley Earl as head of GM Styling, had another SR-2 built with various design updates, many of which were retrofitted to the original Jerry Earl car. Mitchell is pictured opposite with "his" SR-2—note the "zoomie" exhaust pipes, driver canopy, and absence of fender-top and bodyside scoops. The other opposite-page photos depict the restored Earl car. The SR-2 did race duty in 1957 as well; pictured above is an SR-2 pit stop at Sebring, and at right is famed early 'Vette driver Dr. Dick Thompson accompanied by Betty Skelton. Skelton was no stranger to fast 'Vettes—she drove a mildly modified '56 to 145.044 mph at Daytona Beach, setting a new speed record for women. Though the SR-2 wasn't a rousing success in competition, it was the first serious factory-built Corvette race car, and it set the table for future factory racing 'Vettes.

1957 Sebring SS

Conceived in July 1956 with an eye toward the '57 LeMans 24-hour race, the unique Corvette Sebring SS experimental had a super-light magnesium body, advanced tubular space frame, and high-power fuelie V-8. It should have been a world-beater, but it lasted only 23 laps in a warmup run at the April 1957 Sebring 12 hours in Florida before retiring with suspension problems. That would be its only competition appearance, as Chevrolet was forced to abandon the SS program in the wake of Detroit's self-imposed "racing ban" announced that same month. Chevy also entered stock Corvettes in the Sebring race, which finished 1-2 in the GT class and a credible 12th and 15th overall.

1959-1960 Stingray

Stingray/1962 SCCA Corvettes

While production Corvettes continued to dice it up in Sports Car Club of America competition (opposite, top left), newly minted GM design chief Bill Mitchell was crafting the next great Corvette show/race machine: the Stingray. Utilizing the chassis from the 1957 Sebring SS, Mitchell had swoopy new bodywork created that predicted the look of the '63 Sting Ray. The Stingray saw plenty of track action (on Mitchell's own dime, thanks to the racing ban) and was repaired and repainted multiple times. In the top photo, Mitchell stands by the car with racing legend Phil Hill behind the wheel. The 'Vette won its first SCCA B-Production championship in 1962. At middle right, Don Yenko's number 10 and Dr. Dick Thompson's 11 get ready for a three-hour contest at Daytona. At bottom right, Yenko leads a Lister-Chevrolet during the same race.

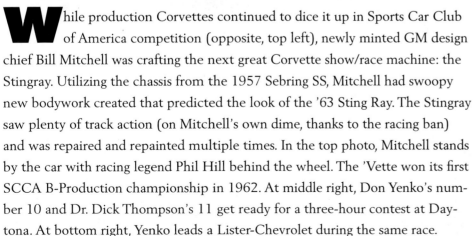

1963 Z06 Corvettes

Chevrolet wasted little time getting the new 1963 Sting Ray into competition. Specially prepped Z06 race cars (this page) debuted at California's Riverside race course in October 1962, alongside another important new sports car: the Ford-powered Cobra roadster of Carroll Shelby. The budding rivalry with the Cobra would overshadow most 'Vette racing efforts for the rest of the decade. The 1963 Grand Sport (opposite) was essentially a GM "skunk works" project that began in 1962. Because of GM's racing ban, Zora Arkus-Duntov and his team had to work secretly. The Grand Sport retained the same basic dimensions as the production Sting Ray, but underwent significant weight-saving measures. Under the hood was an all-aluminum 377-cid small-block V-8 that put out about 550 hp.

1963 Grand Sport

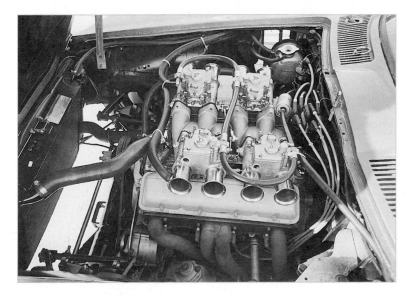

Grand Sport

The Grand Sport was intended to dethrone Carroll Shelby's Cobra as king of production sports-car racing, but angry GM managers prevented that by abruptly canceling the project in 1963. Duntov had planned to build 125 Grand Sports to qualify it as a production sports car, but only five were built before the program was axed. The wily Duntov, however, had the cars sold to favored private owners, who raced them through 1966. Though Grand Sports looked like showroom Sting Rays, their construction and mechanicals were far more exotic. The first two Grand Sports were rebuilt as roadsters for races requiring that body style. The GS never got a true chance to prove itself, but it had all the makings of a world-beating competition car.

1960s-1970s C3 Race Cars

Like previous Corvettes, the new "shark" generation immediately began tearing up American racetracks. Shown clockwise from top left on this page are: a 1969 starting grid (note the Camaro pace car); the 1968 Owens-Corning Fiberglas SCCA A-production-class-winning car; Tony DeLorenzo leading teammate Jerry Thompson at the June 1968 Mid-Ohio SCCA Nationals; and an Owens-Corning team car in pre-race trials at Daytona in 1971. Shown opposite clockwise from top left are: J. Marshall Robbins in Road Atlanta Trans Am action (first two photos) and Mid-Ohio A-production competition in 1973; Jim Meyer in an IMSA Camel GT car at Mid-Ohio in 1975; and Jack Broomhall's B-production C2 roadster in 1979. Thanks to aerodynamic aids, wider tires, and other updates, many 1963-67 'Vettes continued their racing careers well into the 1970s.

1980s-1990s C4 Race Cars

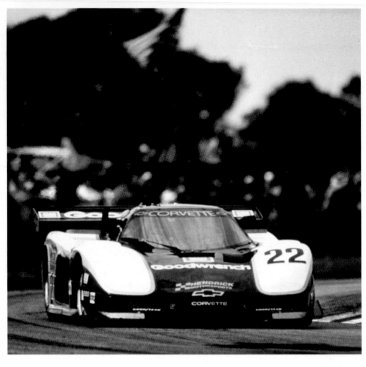

Another new Corvette, another wave of dazzling new competition cars. Opposite, clockwise from top left: The 1984 Corvette represented a quantum leap forward in technology, and of course the new car looked great in competition trim; created for the International Motor Sports Association's GT Prototype class, the Corvette GTP was powered by a midmounted turbocharged V-6 that made more than 1000 hp; at the 1987 Daytona 24-hour race, GM engineer John Heinricy and actor Bobby Carradine helped pilot this IMSA GTO Corvette; Al Unser Jr., Robby Unser, and Bobby Unser drove this 'Vette racer (shown here next to a customized production 'Vette) in the 1987 24 Hours of Mid-Ohio Escort Endurance Race. This page: Corvettes like these so dominated SCCA Showroom Stock racing in the '80s that a 'Vettes-only "Corvette Challenge" series was created.

1999-2002 C5-R

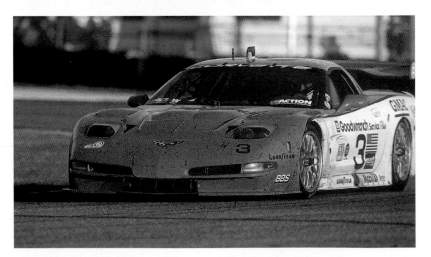

Chevrolet committed to big-league Corvette racing like never before with the introduction of the C5-R in 1999. Competing as a production-based sports car, the C5-R was designed as a GTS-class racer that maintained the integrity of the production Corvette and shared a number of standard-issue components. Success came quickly for the new racing program, thanks in part to some of the best driving talent around. Shown at middle right is the 2001 24 Hours of Daytona winning team of (left to right) Andy Pilgrim, Kelly Collins, Dale Earnhardt, and Dale Earnhardt Jr. The elder Earnhardt was killed in a tragic crash a week later, at the 2001 Daytona 500. At bottom right are the number 63 and 64 C5-R teams that posted a 1-2 finished at the 2002 24 Hours of LeMans—the second time the C5-R had accomplished that feat.

2003-2004 C5-R

The Corvette C5-R enjoyed continued success in 2003 and 2004. The 2003 season cars wore the LeMans Blue with silver/red stripes paint scheme that later showed up on the production 2004 Commemorative Edition Corvettes. The paint scheme reverted to yellow in 2004, when the C5-Rs posted their third 1-2 finish in four years at the 24 Hours of LeMans. The C5-Rs had an impressive run by any measure, but by 2005 a new showroom Corvette meant a new racing version as well. The Corvette C6.R made its competition debut on March 19, 2005, at the Mobil 1 12 Hours of Sebring. CNC-ported cylinder heads and titanium valves and connecting rods helped the C6.R's 7.0-liter V-8 produce about 590 hp and 640 lb-ft of torque. Front fender louvers provided improved brake cooling—an important feature, considering the intense heat the brake rotors must endure in racing.

2005 C6.R

2006-2010 C6.R

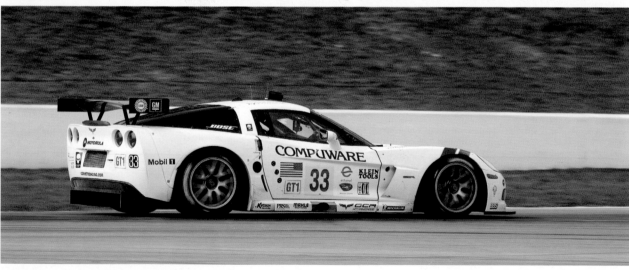

Like its C5-R predecessor, the C6.R was developed by Pratt and Miller Engineering of New Hudson, Michigan. These were true production-based race cars—as the C6.R program progressed, the Corvette Racing team and the production Corvette engineering team worked in close partnership to improve both the track and street 'Vettes. The first generation C6.R was developed alongside the production 2006 Z06. The second-generation C6.R debuted in 2009 and was homologated off of the production 2009 Corvette ZR1. The C6.Rs continued the winning ways of their C5-R predecessors, racking up an impressive string of victories in short order. Shown here are scenes from the 2006-2010 C6.R racing seasons, along with a "family portrait" of the entire team taken in front of the paddock compound at the 2010 12 Hours of Sebring race. Chevrolet's continued commitment to its Corvette Racing program brought new meaning to the old "Win on Sunday, sell on Monday" and "Racing improves the breed" maxims—and provided a new generation of racing enthusiasts with thrilling on-track action.

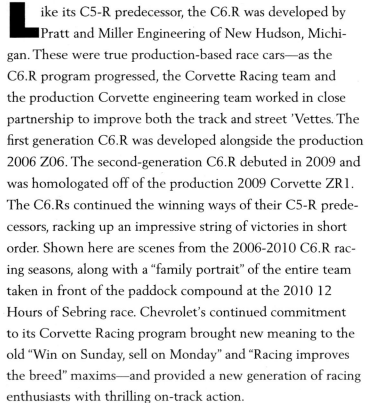

CHAPTER SIX

Powerhouses

From the very first 1953 roadster on, Corvette engines have always represented the pinnacle of GM performance engineering. Though the emissions challenges of the 1970s caused a precipitous drop in power, subsequent technological advances have steadily elevated Corvette horsepower output to previously unimaginable levels. Today's 'Vette engines are marvels of sheer muscle, refinement, and, yes, efficiency.

Below left and right:
Triple carbs, a more-radical camshaft, high-compression heads, and other tweaks helped the Corvette version of Chevy's six make 150 hp.

Left: *The 1955 Corvette got the hottest version of Chevrolet's brand-new V-8. Thanks to a four-barrel carb and a special camshaft, it produced 195 horsepower.* **Above:** *For '56, an available dual-quad version of the 'Vette's V-8 produced up to 240 hp.*

Above: *Made by GM's Rochester Carburetor Division, 1957's mechanical fuel-injection system used a special two-piece aluminum manifold casting.*

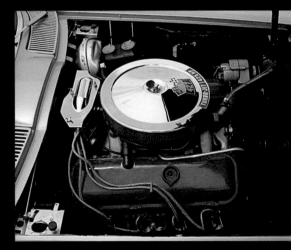

Above: *For 1962, the 283 V-8 grew to 327 cubic inches. Dual carbs weren't available this year, but the top four-barrel made 340 hp.* **Right:** *Choosing the 360-hp fuel-injected engine added $430.40 to the cost of a '63 'Vette.*

Above: *Big-block power arrived in mid-1965 in the form of Chevy's new 396-cid Turbo Jet. The 396 came in just one version: a solid-lifter, 11.0:1-compression brute with 425 horsepower.*

Above: *Fuel injection was discontinued for 1966, but the optional big block grew from 396 cubic inches to 427. Initially assessed at 450 horsepower, the top 427 V-8 was later downrated to 425 hp. The engines themselves weren't changed; Chevrolet was likely trying to mollify increasingly nervous insurance companies.*

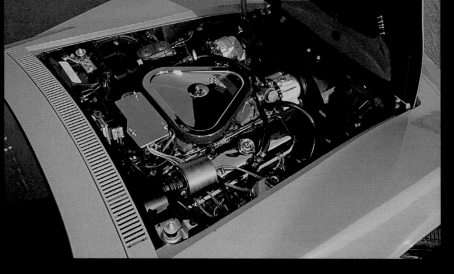

Above: *A triple-carbed version of the 427 was available in 1967, '68, and '69 with either 400 or 435 horsepower.* **Right:** *One of the rarest Corvette engines ever is the ultra-exotic, aluminum-block ZL1 of 1969. Records show only two ZL1 Corvettes were built at the factory. One reason for the rarity was price—with the necessary options, the ZL1 cost more than the 'Vette itself!*

Above: *Big blocks got bigger still for 1970, growing to 454 cubic inches, though peak horsepower actually dropped to 390.* **Right:** *Though 1971 marked the beginning of the end for unfettered V-8 muscle, Chevy still offered a 425-hp LS6 454.*

Above: *By 1974, the mighty 454 was down to 270 horsepower, while the top small-block 350 had slipped to 250 hp.*

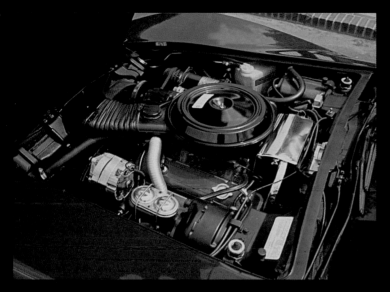

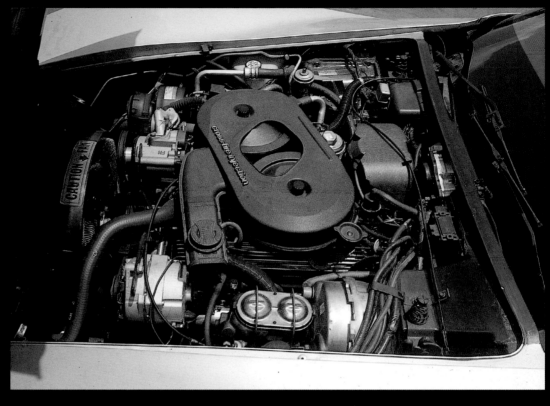

Above: *After bottoming out in 1975, horsepower was on the rise again in '76. The base 350 made 180 hp, while the optional L82 made 210.*

Right: *Cross-Fire Injection debuted on the 1982 Corvette (shown) and was carried over to the new 1984 C4. Carburetors were now history.*

Left: *More-sophisticated Tuned Port Injection debuted for 1985, complete with a slick-looking aluminum intake plenum with tuned intake runners.*
Above: *The mighty ZR-1 5.7-liter LT5 V-8 was unleashed for 1990 with 375 horsepower.*

Above: *Dual overhead camshafts, 32 valves, distributor-less coil ignition, forged crankshaft and con-rods, and tight 11.25:1 compression were just a few of the LT5's high-performance features.*

Above: *The stalwart 5.7-liter V-8 was thoroughly reworked for 1992 to become the 300-horsepower LT1, which topped the previous L98 by 50 hp.* **Right:** *The new-for-1996 330-hp LT4 (shown) was exclusive to manual-transmission Corvettes. Automatics were limited to the LT1.*

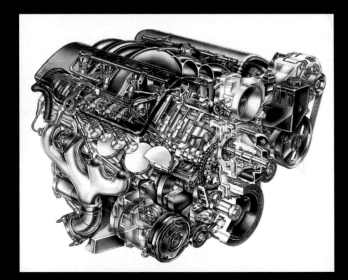

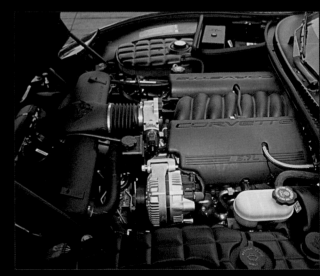

Power for the 1997 C5 Corvette came from a clean-sheet redesign of the pushrod small block dubbed LS1. Fully dressed, it weighed 45 pounds less than the LT4, yet made 15 more horsepower.

An overhead-cam design was initially considered for the 1997 C5 engine, but it couldn't be made short enough to clear the car's low hoodline.

The 2001 Z06's LS6 V-8 made 385 horsepower and could be identified by its red plastic cylinder-head covers. For 2002, the LS6's hp rating was boosted to 405.

Above: *By 2002, output of the base LS1 engine had inched up to 350 horsepower.* **Right:** *The 2005 C6 'Vette's 6.0-liter LS2 upped the hp ante to 400. It was essentially a bored-out version of the aluminum-block 5.7-liter LS1 that debuted in the 1997 C5.*

Above: *The 2006 Z06's LS7 displaced 7.0 liters or, more nostalgically, 427 cubic inches—the same size as the classic big-block 1966-1969 Corvettes. It was rated at an impressive 505 horsepower.*

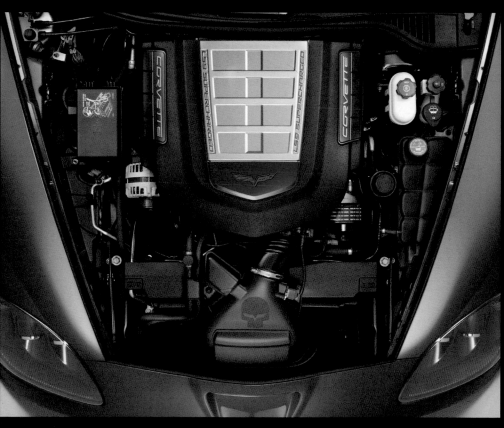

Left: *The 2009-2010 ZR1's 638-hp supercharged 6.2-liter LS9 seemed destined to be the ultimate high-water mark for 'Vette muscle. Note the crossed-flags skull insignia on the air intake box—this logo, named "Jake," was the mascot for the Racing team.* **Above:** *Base 2010 Corvettes and Grand Sports came standard with the 430-hp LS3 V-8.*

CHAPTER SEVEN

Pace Cars and Special Editions

The Corvette was 25 years old before it finally served as official pace car for the famous Indianapolis 500 race in 1978. Chevrolet capitalized on the occasion by offering special-edition replicas to the public, and in doing so created huge excitement among car enthusiasts and collectors. The company realized it had a profitable formula on its hands, and a steady flow of special limited-production 'Vettes followed in the ensuing years. Each boasted unique trim and features that celebrated anniversaries, honored Corvette racers, or simply added some exclusive cachet. Meanwhile, it became readily apparent that Chevy's sports car was virtually tailor-made for the specific needs of pace-car duty, and Corvette gradually became the pace car of choice for major-league racing.

A Corvette Indy Pace Car family portrait, circa 2005: The C5 'Vette Indy Pace Car takes center stage on the famed "Brickyard" with its six predecessors.

1978

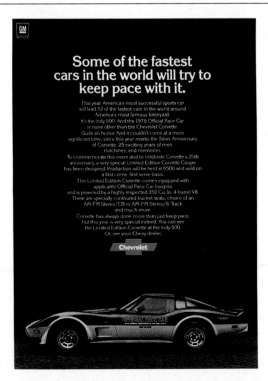

Corvette's 25th anniversary arrived in 1978, and Chevrolet celebrated in high style. Surprisingly, America's sports car had not yet served as the official pace car for the greatest spectacle in racing, a situation remedied by a classy, specially trimmed '78 Vette. Chevy offered limited-edition replicas for sale—at $13,653, they listed for a whopping $4300 over the base coupe, and some buyers paid more than that. Production was initially set at 2500, but eventually ballooned past 6500, making it not particularly "limited" after all. Also offered on '78 'Vettes was a $399 Silver Anniversary Paint package that consisted of a subtle two-tone silver finish split by a thin pinstripe. For 1982, Chevrolet gave the long-serving "Shark" a proper send-off with a special Collector Edition. It featured silver-beige metallic paint with fade-away panels on the hood and body sides, unique wheels, and a flip-up glass rear window. At $22,538, it was the first 'Vette to crack the $20K barrier.

1978, 1982

The Silver Anniversary Corvette.

25 years of men, machines, and memories.

It stands alone today as it has since the summer of 1953, a truly unique and finely machined two-seater. America's only true production sports car.

The legend lives on and improves, as legends do, with the passage of time.

The Silver Anniversary Corvette: Twenty-five years in the making, and we've enjoyed every minute of it.

And now, if you will, please join us in a round of applause for the Corvette founding fathers, that spirited corps of doers and dreamers who created the legend, brought it to life, and kept it there.

Also for the countless men and women who've had a hand in building and refining Corvettes over the years. For everyone who has ever owned a Corvette, driven one, loved one. Or dreamed about owning one someday.

Which, we'd imagine, includes just about everybody.

SEE WHAT'S NEW TODAY IN A CHEVROLET.

Chevrolet

1986, 1988

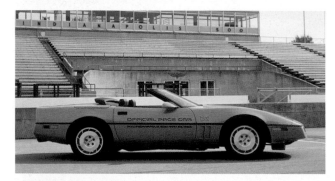

1992-1993

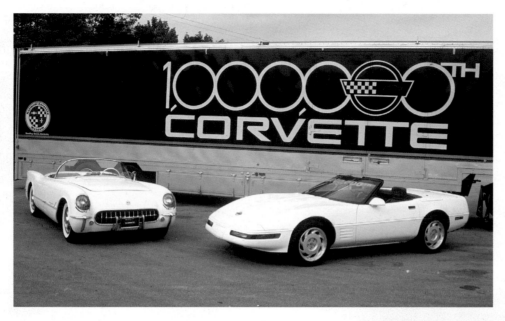

Famed pilot Chuck Yeager drove the 1986 Corvette Indy Pace Car, which helped celebrate the return of a 'Vette ragtop. For 1988, a 35th Special Edition Package was offered on all coupes for a cool $4795; it included "white-out" body trim with a black roof, special badges, and a white leather interior. Corvette hit a major milestone on July 2, 1992, with the production of the one-millionth 'Vette. Chief engineers Zora Arkus-Duntov (left) and Dave McClellan were on hand for the occasion. Another anniversary edition was rolled out for the Corvette's 40th in 1993, and it was available on any model. Exclusive Ruby Red paint, matching leather seats, 40th anniversary badges, and color-keyed wheel centers were all part of the $1455 package.

We Should All Look This Good At Forty.

1995

A Corvette paced the Indianapolis 500 for the third time in 1995, and about 500 replicas—all convertibles—were duly offered to the public. The package cost $2816 and included ZR-1 wheels and two-tone leather sport seats with the Indy 500 logo embroidered on the headrests. For 1996, Chevrolet trotted out two special editions to mark the end of the C4. The Grand Sport revived the name and spirit of the famed '63 race car; it featured an Admiral Blue paint scheme with a white dorsal stripe and red hash marks and, on coupes, wider rear tires with add-on fender flares. The Collector Edition included exclusive Sebring Silver paint and badging.

1996

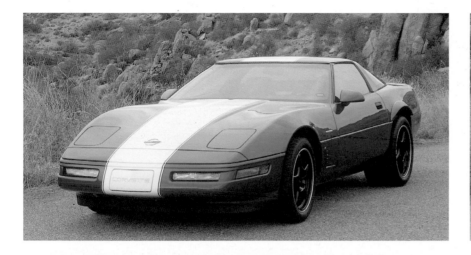

1998

1999-2000

A 1998 convertible was the 11th Chevrolet and the fourth Corvette to pace the Indianapolis 500. Deep purple paint was set off by striking yellow wheels, a colorful graphics package, and yellow-trimmed interior. Chevy sold 1163 replicas to the public at a hefty $5039 premium ($5804 with manual transmission), but only the actual pace car had a "double bubble" strobe-light/roll bar behind the seats. Coinciding with the inauguration of the C5-R racing program, a pair of specially equipped C5 hardtops served as pace cars for the 1999 running of the 24 Hours of LeMans in France. The unmistakable "checkered ribbon" paint scheme was also used on the 1999 Rolex 24 Hours at Daytona pace car. Save for chrome wheels, custom exhaust, and the obligatory auxiliary lights, these pace cars were stock. For 2000, the 'Vette reprised its pace-car role at the Daytona 24 hour race, this time with a Millennium Yellow coupe wearing polished examples of the 'Vette's new thin-spoke wheels.

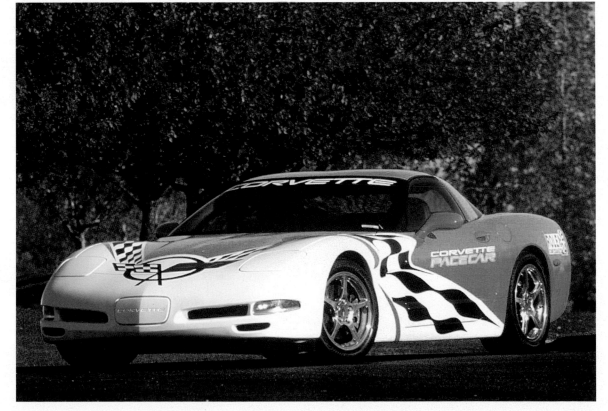

2002

2003

Corvette's Golden Anniversary celebration began in April 2002 with word that a 2003 coupe would pace the 2002 Indianapolis 500. Chevrolet had a great day all-around during that 86th running of the Memorial Day Classic—Team Penske driver Helio Castroneves scored his second straight Indy 500 win, piloting a Chevy-powered Dallara. Except for the pace car graphics, the special appearance features of the 2002 pace car were passed on to the 2003 50th Anniversary Special Edition Corvettes. Available on coupes and convertibles for an extra $5000, the package included a handsome metallic-burgundy Anniversary Red exterior with champagne-colored wheels and specific badges. Inside, a shale interior was highlighted with embroidered emblems on the seats and floormats. Also included was the 'Vette's new Magnetic Selective Ride Control suspension.

2004

With the new C6 Corvette on-track for its debut as a 2005 model, Chevrolet issued the expected special-edition trim package to close out the C5's impressive run. It was called the Commemorative Package, appropriately enough, and included special emblems and LeMans Blue paint with silver/red stripes—a scheme that mimicked the successful 2003 C5-R race cars. The package retailed for $3700 on Corvette coupes and convertibles and $4335 on the Z06 hardtop, where it added a few extra features including an exclusive carbon-fiber hood. Also in 2004, the 'Vette returned to Indy for another go-around as official pace car, this time with a star-spangled red, white, and blue color scheme. Celebrated actor Morgan Freeman (shown above) handled the driving duties, but Chevrolet elected not to offer pace car replicas to the public this year.

2005

The introduction of the C6 Corvette for 2005 seemed to up Chevrolet's pace-car pace. Former U.S. Secretary of State General Colin Powell took the wheel of the 2005 Indy Pace Car Corvette ragtop for the 89th running of the race on May 29, 2005. Earlier that year, a 2005 coupe took to the high banks of Daytona International Speedway to pace the NASCAR Nextel Cup Daytona 500. Though these two pace cars featured a similar graphics scheme, the Indy car was finished in Victory Red and the Daytona car wore Millennium Yellow. Opposite: Not surprisingly, the new-for-2006 Corvette Z06 got into the pace-car act right away. The 2006 Daytona 500 Z06 wore a wild white-to-purple gradated-scallop paint scheme, and the 2006 Indy 500 pace car joined the ever-growing family of Corvette and Chevrolet Indianapolis 500 pace vehicles.

2006

2007

Pace-car proliferation continued in 2007. Pictured opposite are baseball legend Cal Ripken Jr. giving the thumbs-up from behind the wheel of the 2007 Z06 Daytona 500 pace car before the start of the race; the checkerboard-painted Z06 of the NASCAR Allstate 400 at the Brickyard race; and actor/race-car driver Patrick Dempsey with the 2007 Indianapolis 500 pace car. After taking a few seasons off, Chevrolet returned to the Indy pace-car replica business this year, offering 500 production examples at $66,995, or $68,245 with the optional paddle-shift automatic. The Z06 got its own limited-production special for 2007 too: the Ron Fellows ALMS GT1 Championship edition. Named after the successful Canadian driver for the Corvette Racing team, the Fellows Z06 wore Arctic White paint with red hash marks and an armrest signed and numbered by Fellows. The base price was $77,500, and production was limited to just 399.

2008

Chevrolet employed two different Corvettes to pace the 2008 Indianapolis 500: a ragtop and a special one-off Z06 equipped to run on E85 ethanol-blend fuel and finished in color-shifting green-gold paint. The pace Z06 was not available as a production model, but replicas of the black and silver car were offered in both coupe and convertible form. The 2008 pace car marked the 10th time the Corvette paced the Indy 500, and also commemorated the 30th anniversary of the original '78 Corvette pace car. The 2008 Daytona 500 and Allstate 400 at the Brickyard again got their own one-off Z06 pace cars with eye-assaulting paint schemes, and another limited-production Z06 special was released: the 427 Limited Edition. Intended as a nostalgic throwback to the 427-powered 'Vettes of yore, the package included special Crystal Red paint and interior trim, chrome wheels, and unique graphics. Just 505 were built.

2009

'Z51 and Z06 versions available'

Two more special-edition appearance packages were announced for 2009, and both traded heavily on the C6.R's racing heritage. Available on all '09 'Vettes except the ZR1, the GT1 Championship Edition featured either black or Velocity Yellow paint, the latter complemented by black headlight bezels. C6.R-inspired graphics included "Jake," the Corvette Racing skull mascot. The Competition Sport package was limited to coupes and Z06s; it added such features as Competition Gray stripes, wheels, and headlight bezels, plus racing-style numbers based on build sequence for the customer to apply. On May 28, 2009, the 1.5-millionth Corvette rolled off the assembly line, giving Chevrolet a much-needed cause for celebration in a rather bleak economic climate.

2011

Just as the 2010 Grand Sport bridged the gap between the base Corvette and Z06, the 2011 Z06 Carbon Limited Edition was set to split the difference between a Z06 and the line-topping ZR1. In addition to the expected unique trim pieces and badging, Carbon's ZR1-level functional features included carbon-fiber body parts, Brembo carbon-ceramic brakes, and sinister-looking black 20-spoke wheels on Michelin PS2 tires. Just two color choices were available: Inferno Orange and Supersonic Blue. Both came with color-matched interior stitching and racing numbers that could be applied by the customer for track-day events. Chevrolet announced that Carbon Edition production would be limited to 500, but that the mechanical upgrades would be available for 2011 Z06 'Vettes as an optional Z07 performance package.

CHAPTER EIGHT

The Hot Seat

For a sports-car aficionado, there are few places more inviting than the driver's seat of a Corvette. From the beginning, Corvette cockpits always aimed to offer a cutting-edge blend of all-American performance and style, all while catering to the desires of driving enthusiasts. Today's Corvettes deliver unprecedented levels of technology, comfort, and refinement, but remain 100-percent true to the brand's storied heritage.

Below left: *The '53 dash had an attractive "dual-cove" design.* **Below right:** *The 1956-57 interior was little changed overall, save for a racier steering wheel.*

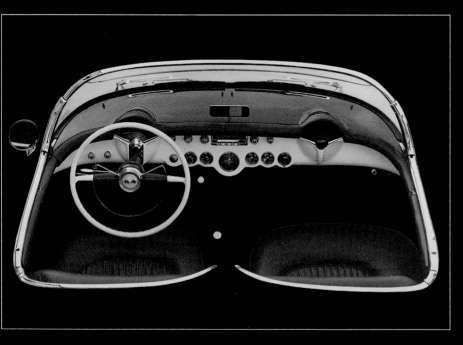

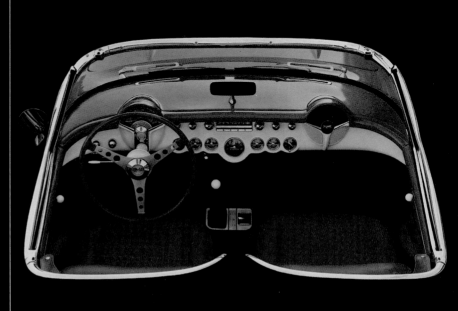

Left: *A passenger grab bar and more-ergonomic gauge cluster debuted for 1958.* **Right:** *A close-up of a 1961 gauge cluster.* **Below:** *Except for minor details, 1962 interiors hadn't changed much since 1958.*

Left: *The all-new 1963 Sting Ray interior retained the familiar dual-cowl design and driver-focused instruments, but with a more-modern look. Gauges had unique bright-finished center "funnels."* **Right:** *The 1965 interiors got new gauges, walnut-finished steering wheels, and other minor updates.*

Above: *The all-new cockpit for 1968 featured space-age styling with a central control panel, but some buyers complained of cramped interior space.* **Below:** *Changes for 1969 included dual map pockets to compensate for the lack of a glove box and thinner door panels for more room.*

Left: *Horizontal seat pleats, a new addition for mid-'71, continued for 1975. The 'Vette convertible would go on an extended hiatus after this year.* **Above:** *Leather seats were standard for 1977, but a cloth/leather combination could be substituted at no cost.*

Left: *Thanks to regular updates over the years, the basic "Shark" dashboard still looked reasonably modern for 1981.* **Above and below:** *Chevrolet went "full-techno" for the groundbreaking 1984 Corvette interior. Not everyone adored the graduated-color, 85-mph speedometer and tachometer or their matching digital readouts. Digital gauges at the center included readouts for range and fuel economy.*

Right: *A rounded, cockpit-style dashboard with both digital and analog gauges debuted for 1990. A 1991 model is shown here.* **Far right:** *ZR-1 interiors, like this swan-song 1995 model, differed little from their lesser counterparts.* **Below:** *The C5 Corvette debuted for 1997 with a new iteration of the traditional "twin cowl" dash. Full analog instrumentation was welcomed by most enthusiasts.*

Above: *The new-for-2001 Z06 sported special black-and-red upholstery, more heavily bolstered seats, and embroidered Z06 logos.* **Below:** *Like other C5 Corvettes, the Z06's speedometer readout went to 200 mph... a far cry from the 85-mph maximum of the 1984 'Vette speedo.*